Understanding Supreme Court Better

101 facts you need to know...

Compiled by

lawinc

Law Information Center
'LawCon House', D-61, East of Kailash, New Delhi - 110065
Tel: 91 11 46579779; Fax: 91 11 26447191,
Web: *http://www.lawinc.in*
Email - lawinformationcentre@gmail.com

Published by
Originals
A-6, Nimri Commercial Centre,
Near Ashok Vihar Phase-IV, Delhi-110052
Phones: 27302453
e-mail: info@Lppindia.com
Website: www.Lppindia.com

First Published 2010

ISBN 10: 81-8454-102-3
ISBN 13: 978-81-8454-102-1

Printed at
D K Fine Art Press P Ltd.
Delhi-110052

PRINTED IN INDIA

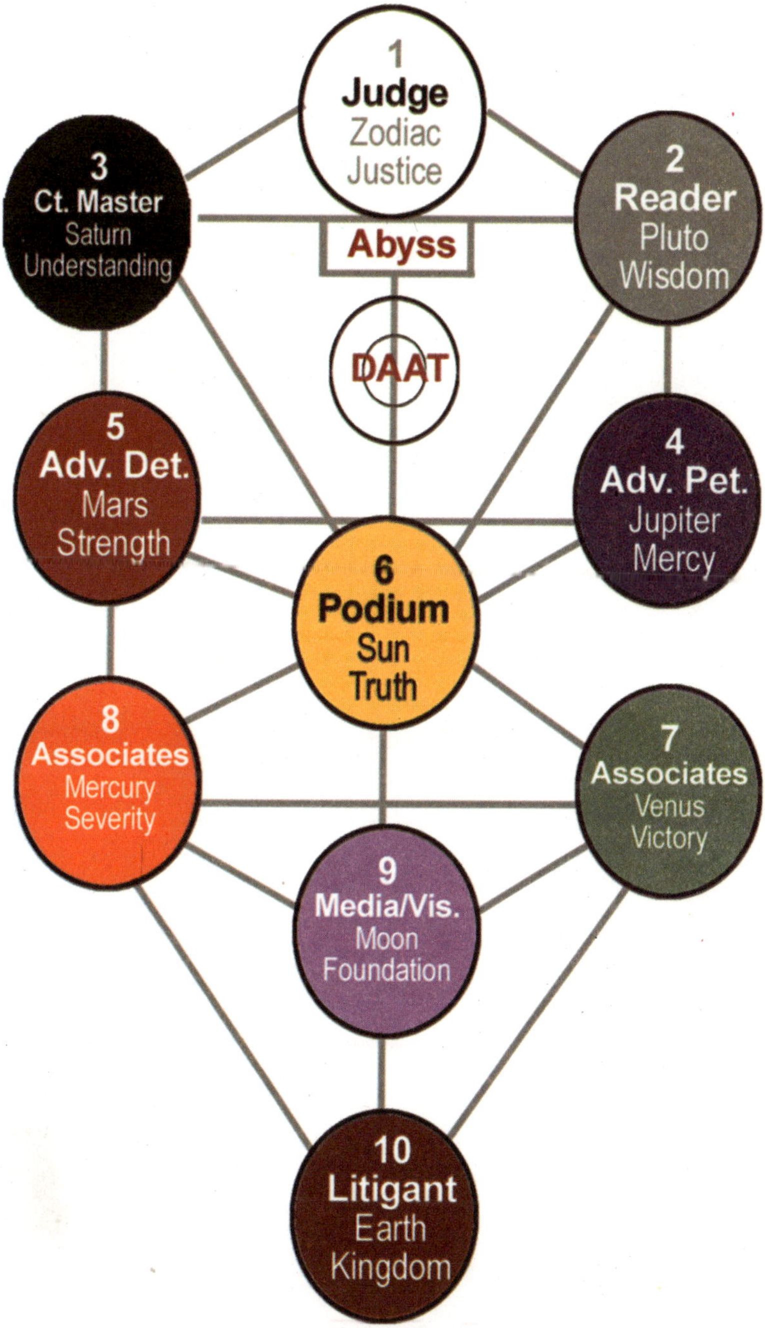
1
Judge
Zodiac
Justice
3
Ct. Master
Saturn
Understanding
2
Reader
Pluto
Wisdom
Abyss
DAAT
5
Adv. Det.
Mars
Strength
4
Adv. Pet.
Jupiter
Mercy
6
Podium
Sun
Truth
8
Associates
Mercury
Severity
7
Associates
Venus
Victory
9
Media/Vis.
Moon
Foundation
10
Litigant
Earth
Kingdom

Contents

Hon'ble Justice Altamas Kabir,
Judge, Supreme Court of India

Foreword

This compilation for '*Understanding the Supreme Court Better*" is a unique collection of information which is not within the knowledge of most people, not even some of us Judges. Some of the information provides an insight into the working of the Supreme Court and its judges ever since it came into existence.

However, all the information provided in the compilation are judge-based and I am sure that in future the editors of the compilation may consider adding some information as to the development of various aspects of the law which came to be interpreted by the Supreme Court at different points of time of its existence. Certain eras of the Court's history can be definitely identified as periods during which new ground was broken in relation to labour and service-oriented matters and also tenancy matters, in the interest of social justice. Yet another era can be identified with the intervention of the Supreme Court relating to human rights violations and the right to life and liberty of citizens guaranteed under the Constitution. This was at a time when the Supreme Court was at its creative best, breathing life into the otherwise insipid provisions of Article 21 of the Constitution, to bring within its embrace transgressions by the State authorities of human, basic and fundamental rights of the citizens of this country and other individuals. Interesting anecdote and witty repartees during court proceedings, is another area which can be explored.

I commend the efforts put in by all those who are connected with the preparation of the compilation and I sincerely hope that the same will be kept updated in future with new ideas and related information.

Altamas Kabir

Hon'ble Justice Arijit Pasayat
Chairman, Law Information Center

Preface

"Understanding Supreme Court Better" is a goldmine (or shall I say diamond mine) of illuminating, informative and interesting information. Some of the details given have never in the past seen the light of day. There is a touch of novelty when one goes back in time. The compilation not only refers to "101 Facts You Need To Know" but also much more. It has rightly highlighted how data accumulation helps in national growth. Lots of hard work with meticulous precision has resulted in this unique compilation.

It would be appropriate if the data gets annually updated by bringing out an annual supplement and a new compilation every five years. The Law Information Centre can explore the possibility of bringing out similar compilations in respect of every High Court. I have no doubt that this compilation shall make anyone who reads it understand the Supreme Court better.

The compilation amply reflects the tremendous work done by the Judges of Supreme Court in dealing with matters coming before it.

Dr. Justice Arijit Pasayat

Introduction

Supreme Court of India is the most powerful, dynamic and effective institution of the largest democracy in the world. From the day it was inaugurated on January 28, 1950 till May 14, 2010 Supreme Court has worked for 60 yrs and 1 term totaling to 121 terms. During this period 195 judges have been elevated to the Supreme Court, out of which 29 are presently sitting judges. These are some of the facts and statistics about Supreme Court and 195 Hon'ble Judges of Supreme Court, who have vigilantly read, heard, considered and taken decisions in about 1.35 million petitions/ appeals filed during this period. The information provided in this compilation is based on an analysis of 39,657 judgments and orders (reportable and non - reportable) delivered during this period. The enormous amount of work undertaken by Supreme Court, while maintaining the highest dignity, decorum and distinction is unique and amazing and has no match, parallel or comparison, with any other apex court in the world. During this period Supreme Court has worked for about 11,285 days and a total number of 356,401 judge days.

Law Information Center is presenting this compilation with great awe, admiration, esteem and respect for a great institution, which has held its head high and that of a great culture, tradition and heritage - India, that is Bharat.

Note:

1. Great care and all possible efforts have been made to precisely update the data to the best of the abilities. However, unconsciously and due to inaccuracy in information, some serious or some not so serious errors may have crept in the data and compilation of the data. Such errors would be totally inadvertent, unintentional and bonafide. Law Information Center takes full responsibility for such errors and seeks indulgence and apology for such errors. Any person who comes across any such errors may immediately report to Law Information Center, so that the subsequent editions would be corrected to that extent. Thanks for support and encouragement.
2. Hon'ble Justice Ramachander Naik and Hon'ble Justice Khaleeluzzaman Siddiqui, who have been members of 4 judgments each, of Supreme Court of India (Hyderabad) were appointed in 1950 as ad-hoc judges of Supreme Court, to dispose appeals which were pending before the than Privy Council at Hyderabad. The name of these two Hon'ble Judges, whose judgments are reported in Supreme Court Reports, the official law reports series, do not find place in the official list of judges of Supreme Court of India and as such there will be difference in the data maintained by Supreme Court with respect to number of Judges and Law Information Center.
3. Some data relating to sitting judges have not been included in the listing of some information, because they have miles to go...

President, Law Information Center

Understanding Supreme Court Better

1.	Number of Hon'ble Judges:	195
2.	Number of Chief Justices of India:	38
3.	Number of puisne Judges:	157
4.	Chief Justice of India with less than 1 yr. tenure:	16
5.	Chief Justice of India between 1 to 2 yrs. tenure:	10
6.	Chief Justice of India between 2 to 3 yrs. tenure:	6
7.	Chief Justice of India between 3 to 4 yrs. tenure:	5
8.	Chief Justice of India more than 4 yrs.:	1
9.	Number of Hon'ble judges resigned:	7
10.	Number of Hon'ble judges expired in office:	11
11.	Hon'ble Ad-hoc judges for particular cases:	2
12.	Number of Ad-hoc judges:	5
13.	Hon'ble Judges with less than 3 yrs tenure:	34
14.	Hon'ble Judges between 3- 5 yrs tenure:	68
15.	Hon'ble Judges between 5 to 7 yrs. tenure:	49
16.	Hon'ble Judges between 7 to 10 yrs tenure:	36
17.	Hon'ble Judges more than 10 yrs. tenure:	8

18. Judges with longest tenure as Chief Justice of India -

		Days
a.	Y.V.Chandrachud	2690
b.	B.P.Sinha	1584
c.	A.N.Ray	1373
d.	S.R.Dass	1338
e.	K.G.Balakrishnan	1214

19. Judges with shortest tenure as Chief Justice of India -

a.	K.N.Singh	17
b.	S.R.Babu	30
c.	J.C.Shah	36
d.	G.B.Pattnaik	41
e.	L.M.Sharma	86

20. Judges with longest tenure as puisne judge and never became Chief Justice of India -

a.	Syed M.Fazal Ali	3793
b.	A.P.Sen	3717
c.	A.K.Sarkar	3404
d.	O.Chinappa Reddy	3356
e.	Syed Jafar Imam	3308

21. Judges with longest tenure as puisne Judge before becoming Chief Justice of India-

		Days
a.	P.N.Bhagwati	4377
b.	J.C.Shah	4083
c.	E.S.Venkataramiah	3755
d.	S.P.Barucha	3410
e.	M.Hidayatullah	3372

22. Judges with shortest tenure as puisne judge before becoming Chief Justice of India-

a.	M.Patanjali Shastri	284
b.	A.N.Ray	1363
c.	M.C.Mahajan	1438
d.	M.H.Kania	1686
e.	B.K.Mukherjea	1791

23. Judges with longest tenure as judge of Supreme Court -

a.	P.N.Bhagwati	4904
b.	Y.V.Chandrachud	4700
c.	M.Hidayatullah	4398
d.	R.S.Pathak	4136
e.	J.C.Shah	4119

24. Judges with shortest tenure as judge of Supreme Court (incomplete tenure)

		Days
a.	S.C.Roy	116
b.	R.Satyanarayan Raju	182
c.	R.C.Patnaik	192
d.	Saiyid Fazal Ali	358
e.	P.Govind Menon	408

25. Judges with shortest tenure as judge of Supreme Court (complete tenure)

a.	A.Alagiriswami	1095
b.	P.K.I.Baasubramanian	1096
c.	N.Venkatachala	1097
d.	K.S.Paripoornan	1097
e.	N.D.Ojha	1097

26. Judges who had the longest tenure as a judge of High Court before elevation to Supreme Court:

a.	Ashok K. Mathur	7026
b.	N.P.Singh	7004
c.	V.Ramaswami - II	6823
d.	S.P.Kurdukar	6548
e.	S.Mohan	6431

27. Judges who had the shortest tenure as a judge of High Court before elevation to Supreme Court:

		Days
a.	V.R.Krishna Iyer	1841
b.	M.S.Fatima Bibi	2255
c.	A.Algiriswami	2259
d.	R.S.Sarkaria	2288
e.	P.K.Goswami	2313

28. Judges with maximum age before elevation as judges of High Court

a.	M.S.Fatima Bibi	20550
b.	A.Alagiriswami	20387
c.	P.K.Goswami	19854
d.	Bahrul Islam	19683
e.	Jaswant Singh	19393

29. Judges with minimum age before elevation as judges of High Court

a.	Syed M.Fazal Ali	13623
b.	R.S.Pathak	13824
c.	Dr.A.S.Anand	14085
d.	P.N.Bhagwati	14092
e.	J.S.Verma	14482

30. Judges with longest tenure at the Bar before elevated as judges of High Court

		Days
a.	M.S. Fatima Bibi	11951
b.	A.Alagiriswami	11105
c.	V.R.Krishna Iyer	10879
d.	N.Rajagopla Ayyanger	10737
e.	A.Vardharajan	10397

31. Judges with shortest tenure at thc Bar before elevated as judges of High Court

a.	Dr.A.S.Anand	3850
b.	K.N.Singh	4738
c.	J.S.Verma	4773
d.	Syed M.Fazal Ali	4900
e.	A.M.Ahmadi	5004

32. Judges who have been member of highest number of judgments and orders:

		Number
a.	Arijit Pasayat	2661
b.	K.Ramaswamy	2272
c.	S.B.Sinha	2130
d.	J.C.Shah	1845
e.	G.B.Patnaik	1347

33. Judges who have been member of minimum number of Judgments and Orders of Courts (incomplete tenure) Number

a.	Ramachander Naik	4
b.	Khaleeluzzaman Siddiqui	4
c.	S.C.Roy	20
d.	R.C.Patnaik	40
e.	A.K.Mukherjea	42

34. Judges who has been member of minimum number of Judgments and Orders of Courts (complete tenure - 3 yrs or more)

a.	D.P.Madon	112
b.	M.Patanjali Shastri	159
c.	Gulam Hassan	165
d.	T.K.Thommen	165
e.	M.Srinivasan	174

35. Judges who have delivered highest number of Judgments and Orders of Court:

a.	Arijit Pasayat	2197
b.	S.B.Sinha	1593
c.	J.C.Shah	618
d.	Sayed M.Fazal Ali	490
e.	P.B.Gajendragadkar	432

36. Judges who have delivered minimum number of Judgments and Orders of Court (incomplete tenure):

		Number
a.	Ramachander Naik	1
b.	Khaleeluzzaman Siddiqui	1
c.	R.C.Patnaik	1
d.	P.Govind Menon	15
e.	K.Satyanarayan Raju	15

37. Judges who have delivered minimum number of Judgments and Orders of Court (complete tenure):

a.	Gulam Hasan	27
b.	V.Ramaswamy II	31
c.	A.N.Sen	32
d.	D.P.Madon	37
e.	N.D.Oza	42

38. Judges who have delivered highest number of dissenting opinions:

a.	K.Subba Rao	36
b.	A.K.Sarkar	22
c.	M.Hidayattulah	21
d.	Raghubar Dayal	14
e.	J.R.Madholkar	14
f.	K.K.Mathew	14

39. Number of judges who have never delivered a dissenting opinion: 111

40. Number of judges who have delivered 1 dissenting opinion: 21

41. Number of judges who have delivered 2 dissenting opinion: 22

42. Number of judges who have delivered 3 dissenting opinion: 7

43. Number of judges who have delivered 4 dissenting opinion: 9

44. Number of judges who have delivered 5 dissenting opinion: 6

45. Number of judges who have delivered 6 dissenting opinion: 4

46. Number of judges who have delivered 7 dissenting opinion: 2

47. Number of judges who have delivered 8 dissenting opinion: 2

48. Number of judges who have delivered 9 dissenting opinion: 1

49. Number of judges who have delivered 10 dissenting opinion: 3

50. Number of judges who have delivered 11 -15 dissenting opinion: 4

51. Number of judges who have delivered 20 - 25 dissenting opinion: 2

52. Number of judges who have delivered more than 35 dissenting opinion: 1

53. Judges who have delivered highest number of orders:

a.	K.Ramaswamy	1172
b.	K.G.Balakrishnan	305
c.	Y.K.Sabarwal	284
d.	Tarun Chatterjee	247
e.	S.P.Bharucha	246

54. Number of judges who have never passed an order: 62
55. Number of judges who have passed 1 to 10 orders: 45
56. Number of judges who have passed 11 to 20 orders: 20
57. Number of judges who have passed 21 to 50 orders: 28
58. Number of judges who have passed 51 to 100 orders: 19
59. Number of judges who have passed 101 to 200 orders: 15
60. Number of judges who have passed 201 to 300 orders: 6
61. Number of judges who have passed more than 1100 orders: 1
62. Judges who have been signatory of highest number of judgments:

a.	J.C.Shah	1159
b.	G.B.Pattanik	926
c.	K.N.Wanchoo	836
d.	K.Ramaswamy	789
e.	P.B.Gajendragadkar	759

63. Judges who have been signatory of less than 100 judgments: 28

64. Judges who have been signatory of 100 to 200 judgments: 31

65. Judges who have been signatory of 201 to 300 judgments: 65

66. Judges who have been signatory of 301 to 400 judgments: 35

67. Judges who have been signatory of 401 to 500 judgments: 19

68. Judges who have been signatory of 500 to 1000 judgments: 12

69. Judges who have been signatory to more than 1000 judgments: 1

70. Number of Judges who have been member of more than 2000 judgment: 3

71. Number of judges who have been member of 1000 - 2000 judgment: 5

72. Number of judges who have been member of 800 - 1000 judgment: 11

73. Number of judges who have been member of 600 - 800 judgment: 28

74. Number of judges who have been member of 400 - 600 judgment: 54

75. Number of judges who have been member of 200 - 400 judgment: 61

76. Number of judges who have been member of less than - 200 judgment: 33

77. Number of Judges who have delivered more than 2000 Judgment of Court: 1

78. Number of judges who have delivered between 1000 - 2000 Judgment of Court: 1

79. Number of judges who have delivered between 500 - 1000 Judgment of Court: 1

80. Number of judges who have delivered between 401 - 500 Judgment of Court: 3

81. Number of judges who have delivered between 351 - 400 Judgment of Court: 4

82. Number of judges who have delivered between 301 - 350 Judgment of Court: 4

83. Number of judges who have delivered between 251 - 300 Judgment of Court: 15

84. Number of judges who have delivered between 201 - 250 Judgment of Court: 10

85. Number of judges who have delivered between 151 - 200 Judgment of Court: 26

86. Number of judges who have delivered between 101 - 150 Judgment of Court: 51

87. Number of judges who have delivered between 51 - 100 Judgment of Court: 87

88. Number of judges who have delivered less than 50 Judgments of Court: 40

89. Total number of judgments and orders signed by all the judges 90161

90. Number of judgements and orders delivered by benches of:

a.	13 judges	1
b.	11 judges	9
c.	9 judges	13
d.	7 judges	84
e.	6 judges	25
f.	5 judges	2175
g.	4 judges	516
h.	3 judges	9183
i.	2 judges	27166
j.	1 judge	153

91. In their judgments Supreme Court has referred, considered, explained, distinguished judgments of:

a.	United Kingdom	6561
b.	United States of America	1400
c.	Australia	260
d.	Canada	161
e.	New Zealand	11
f.	Pakistan	5
g.	International Human Rights Commission	2

92. In their judgments Supreme Court has referred, considered, explained, distinguished, over-ruled judgments of India

a.	Federal Court	111
b.	High Courts	13313

93. Number of judgments and orders referred, considered, explained, distinguished, over-ruled etc. 87859

94. Total number of judgments and orders in which 1 or more judgment has been referred, considered, explained, distinguished, over-ruled etc. 17632

95. Total number of judgments and orders which have been referred, considered, explained, distinguished, over-ruled etc.

a.	In 1 judgment	23353
b.	In 2 judgments	5434
c.	In 3 judgments	2424
d.	In 4 judgments	1419
e.	In 5 judgments	946
f.	In 6 - 10 judgments	1830
g.	In 11 - 20 judgments	814
h.	In 21 - 50 judgments	292
i.	In 50 - 100 judgments	34
j.	In more than 101 judgments	2

96. Judgments in which maximum number of judgments have been referred, considered, explained, distinguished, over-ruled etc.

a.	H.H.Keshvanand Bharti Vs. State of Kerala	268
b.	S.P.Gupta Vs. Union of India	173
c.	Kartar Singh Vs. State of Punjab	147
d.	Indira Nehru Gandhi Vs. Raj Narain	133
e.	A.D.M.Jabalpur Vs. S.S.Shukla	127

97. Judgment which has been referred, considered, explained, distinguished, over-ruled etc. in maximum number of judgments:

a.	Maneka Gandhi Vs. Union of India	136
b.	Bengal Immunity Co.Ltd. Vs. State of Bihar	101
c.	H.H.Keshvanand Bharti Vs. State of Kerala	91
d.	A.K.Gopalan Vs. Sate of Madras	88
e.	Bachan Singh Vs. Sate of Punjab	88

98. Number of Indian published Law Reports considered: 451

99. Number of overseas published Law Reports considered:

a.	UK	189
b.	USA	60
c.	Australia	7
d.	Canada	4
e.	Pakistan	1
f.	International Human Rights Commission	2

100. Total number of Central and State Statutes considered: 3580

101. Number of Articles, Sections, Rules, Regulations, Clauses etc. of Act, Rule, Regulation etc. referred - 93350

Annexure 1
Chief Justice of India

Sl.	Judge Name	PHC	Date-Appt	CJI From	CJI To	Ten CJI
1	H.J.Kania	Bombay	26/01/1950	26/01/1950	06/11/1950	284
2	M.Patanjali Sastri	T.N.	26/01/1950	06/11/1950	03/01/1954	1154
3	M.C.Mahajan	P & H	26/01/1950	03/01/1954	22/12/1954	353
4	B.K.Mukherjea	Cal	26/01/1950	22/12/1954	31/01/1956	405
5	S.R.Dass	Cal	26/01/1950	31/01/1956	30/09/1959	1338
6	B.P.Sinha	Patna	03/12/1954	30/09/1959	31/01/1964	1584
7	P.B.Gajendragadkar	Bombay	17/01/1957	31/01/1964	15/03/1966	774
8	A.K.Sarkar	Cal	04/03/1957	15/03/1966	30/06/1966	107
9	K.Subha Rao	A.P.	31/01/1958	30/06/1966	11/04/1967	285
10	K.N.Wanchoo	All	11/08/1958	11/04/1967	24/02/1968	319
11	M.Hidayatullah	Bombay	01/12/1958	24/02/1968	16/12/1970	1026
12	J.C.Shah	Bombay	12/10/1959	16/12/1970	21/01/1971	36
13	S.M.Sikri	Bar	02/03/1964	21/01/1971	25/04/1973	825
14	A.N.Ray	Cal	01/08/1969	25/04/1973	27/01/1977	1373
15	M.H.Beg	All	10/12/1971	27/01/1977	28/02/1978	397
16	Y.V.Chandrachud	Bombay	28/08/1972	28/02/1978	11/07/1985	2690
17	P.N.Bhagwati	Gujarat	17/07/1973	11/07/1985	20/12/1986	527
18	R.S.Pathak	All	20/02/1978	20/12/1986	18/06/1989	911
19	E.S.Venkataramiah	Karnataka	08/03/1979	18/06/1989	17/12/1989	182
20	Sabyasachi Mukharji	Cal	15/03/1983	17/12/1989	25/09/1990	282
21	Ranganath Misra	Orissa	15/03/1983	25/09/1990	25/11/1991	426
22	K.N.Singh	All	10/03/1986	25/11/1991	12/12/1991	17
23	M.H.Kania	Bombay	01/05/1987	12/12/1991	17/11/1992	341
24	L.M.Sharma	Patna	05/10/1987	17/11/1992	11/02/1993	86
25	M.N.Venkatachaliah	Karnataka	05/10/1987	11/02/1993	25/10/1994	621
26	A.M.Ahmadi	Guj.	14/12/1988	25/10/1994	25/03/1997	882
27	J.S.Verma	M.P.	25/03/1991	25/03/1997	18/01/1998	299
28	M.M.Punchhi	P & H	06/10/1989	18/01/1998	10/10/1998	265
29	A.S.Anand,Dr	J & K	18/11/1991	10/10/1998	01/11/2001	1118
30	S.P.Bharucha	Bombay	01/07/1992	01/11/2001	06/05/2002	186
31	B.N.Kirpal	Delhi	11/09/1995	06/05/2002	08/11/2002	186
32	G.B.Pattanaik	Orissa	11/09/1995	08/11/2002	19/12/2002	41
33	V.N.Khare	All	21/03/1997	19/12/2002	02/05/2004	500
34	S.R.Babu	A.P.	25/09/1997	02/05/2004	01/06/2004	30
35	R.C.Lahoti	M.P.	09/12/1998	01/06/2004	01/11/2005	518
36	Y.K.Sabharwal	Delhi	28/01/2000	01/11/2005	14/01/2007	439
37	K.G.Balakrishnan	Kerala	08/06/2000	14/01/2007	12/05/2010	1214
38	S.H.Kapadia	Bombay	18/12/2003	12/05/2010	29/09/2012	871

PHC Permanent High Court; **Ten CJI** Tenure as Chief Justice India

Annexure 2
Hon'ble Judges according to Seniority

Sl.	Judge Name	PHC	Date HCJ	Date SCJ	Date Retd.
1	H.J.Kania	Bombay	19/06/1946	26/01/1950	11/06/1951
2	Saiyid Fazal Ali	Patna	09/06/1947	26/01/1950	1/19/1951
3	M.Patanjali Sastri	Madras	06/12/1947	26/01/1950	1/3/1954
4	M.C.Mahajan	Punjab	05/10/1948	26/01/1950	12/22/1954
5	B.K.Mukherjea	Cal	14/10/1948	26/01/1950	1/31/1956
6	S.R.Dass	Cal	01/12/1942	26/01/1950	01/10/1959
7	R. Naik*	A.P.	DNA	28/08/1950	12/30/1950
8	K. Siddiqui*	A.P.	DNA	28/08/1950	12/30/1950
9	N. C. Aiyar	Madras	DNA	23/09/1950	1/24/1953
10	Vivian Bose	Bombay	1/9/1936	05/03/1951	6/9/1956
11	Ghulam Hasan	All	DNA	01/08/1951	11/5/1954
12	N.H.Bhagwati	Bombay	27/08/1944	08/09/1952	8/7/1959
13	B.Jagannath Das	Orissa	30/10/1951	09/03/1953	27/07/1960
14	T.L.V. Ayyar	Madras	07/07/1951	04/01/1954	11/25/1958
15	B.P.Sinha	Patna	06/01/1943	03/12/1954	01/02/1964
16	Syed Jafar Imam	Patna	01/06/1943	10/01/1955	1/31/1964
17	S.K.Das	Patna	04/11/1944	30/04/1956	03/09/1963
18	P.Govinda Menon	Madras	DNA	03/09/1956	10/16/1957
19	J.L.Kapur	Punjab	06/06/1949	14/01/1957	12/13/1962
20	P.B.Gajendragadkar	Bombay	06/03/1945	17/01/1957	16/03/1966
21	A.K.Sarkar	Cal	25/01/1949	04/03/1957	30/06/1966
22	K.Subha Rao	Madras	22/03/1948	31/01/1958	4/11/1967
23	K.N.Wanchoo	All	17/02/1947	11/08/1958	2/24/1968
24	M.Hidayatullah	Bombay	24/06/1946	01/12/1958	17/12/1970
25	K.C.Das Gupta	Bombay	13/05/1948	24/08/1959	03/01/1965
26	J.C.Shah	Bombay	01/03/1949	12/10/1959	22/01/1971
27	Raghuvar Dayal	All	22/07/1946	27/07/1960	26/10/1965
28	N.R. Ayyangar	Madras	23/11/1953	27/07/1960	15/12/1964
29	J.R.Mudholkar	Bombay	21/06/1948	03/10/1960	7/3/1966
30	S.M.Sikri	Bar	06/01/1957	02/03/1964	25/04/1973
31	R.S.Bachawat	Cal	23/01/1950	07/09/1964	8/1/1969
32	V.Ramaswami - I	Patna	01/11/1947	04/01/1965	30/10/1969
33	R.S. Raju	AP	01/11/1954	20/10/1965	4/20/1966
34	J.M.Shelat	Bombay	06/01/1957	24/02/1966	4/30/1973
35	V.Bhargava	All	01/08/1949	08/08/1966	05/02/1971
36	G.K.Mitter	Cal	24/11/1952	29/08/1966	24/09/1971
37	C.A.Vaidialingam	Kerala	27/03/1957	10/10/1966	6/30/1972
38	K.S.Hegde	Karnataka	26/08/1957	17/07/1967	4/30/1973
39	A.N.Grover	Punjab	10/10/1957	12/02/1968	5/31/1973

Annexure 2

Sl.	Judge Name	PHC	Date HCJ	Date SCJ	Date Retd.
40	A.N.Ray	Cal	23/12/1957	01/08/1969	29/01/1977
41	P.Jaganmohan Reddy	A.P.	25/02/1958	01/08/1969	23/01/1975
42	I.D.Dua	P & H	11/08/1958	01/08/1969	04/10/1972
43	S.C.Roy	Bar		19/07/1971	11/12/1971
44	D.G.Palekar	Bombay	14/10/1961	19/07/1971	04/09/1974
45	H.R.Khanna	Punjab	07/05/1962	22/09/1971	3/12/1977
46	K.K.Mathew	Kerala	05/06/1962	04/10/1971	03/01/1976
47	M.H.Beg	All	11/06/1963	10/12/1971	22/02/1978
48	S.N.Dwivedi	All	12/05/1959	14/08/1972	12/8/1974
49	A.K.Mukherjea	Cal	27/02/1962	14/08/1972	10/23/1973
50	Y.V.Chandrachud	Bombay	19/03/1961	28/08/1972	12/07/1985
51	A.Alagiriswami	Madras	11/08/1966	17/10/1972	10/17/1975
52	P.N.Bhagwati	Guj.	21/07/1960	17/07/1973	21/12/1986
53	V.R.Krishna Iyer	Kerala	02/07/1968	17/07/1973	11/15/1980
54	P.K.Goswami	Gauhati	12/05/1967	10/09/1973	1/1/1978
55	R.S.Sarkaria	P & H	13/06/1967	17/09/1973	1/16/1981
56	A.C.Gupta	Cal	24/02/1964	02/09/1974	01/01/1982
57	N.L.Untwalia	Patna	02/02/1958	02/09/1974	8/1/1980
58	Syed M.Fazal Ali	J & K	08/04/1958	02/04/1975	8/20/1985
59	P.N.Shinghal	Raj.	21/06/1961	11/06/1975	10/15/1980
60	Jaswant Singh	J & K	01/03/1967	23/01/1976	1/25/1979
61	P.S.Kailasam	Madras	20/10/1960	03/01/1977	9/12/1980
62	V.D.Tulzapurkar	Bombay	21/12/1963	30/09/1977	3/8/1986
63	D.A.Desai	Guj.	19/02/1968	30/09/1977	4/8/1985
64	R.S.Pathak	All	01/10/1962	20/02/1978	19/06/1989
65	A.D.Koshal	P & H	28/05/1968	17/07/1978	3/7/1982
66	O.Chinnappa Reddy	A.P.	21/08/1967	17/07/1978	25/09/1987
67	A.P.Sen	M.P.	29/07/1968	17/07/1978	20/09/1988
68	E.S.Venkataramiah	Karnataka	25/06/1970	08/03/1979	18/12/1989
69	Baharul Islam	Gauhati	20/01/1972	04/12/1980	13/01/1983
70	A.Varadarajan	Madras	15/02/1973	10/12/1980	17/08/1985
71	A.N.Sen	Cal	15/11/1965	28/01/1981	01/10/1985
72	V.B.Fradi	Kerala	05/04/1967	30/01/1981	19/06/1987
73	R.B.Misra	All	03/01/1968	30/01/1981	6/14/1986
74	D.P.Madon	Bombay	25/09/1967	15/03/1983	07/04/1986
75	Sabyasachi Mukharji	Cal	31/07/1968	15/03/1983	9/25/1990
76	M.P.Thakkar	Guj.	02/07/1969	15/03/1983	11/3/1988
77	Ranganath Misra	Orissa	04/07/1969	15/03/1983	11/25/1991
78	V.Khalid	Madras	03/04/1972	25/06/1984	01/07/1987
79	G.L.Oza	M.P.	29/07/1968	29/10/1985	12/12/1989
80	B.C.Ray	Cal	10/06/1974	29/10/1985	11/1/1991

Annexure 2

Sl.	Judge Name	PHC	Date HCJ	Date SCJ	Date Retd.
81	M.M.Dutt	Cal	18/09/1969	10/03/1986	10/30/1989
82	K.N.Singh	All	25/08/1970	10/03/1986	13/12/1991
83	S.Natrajan	Madras	15/02/1973	10/03/1986	10/29/1989
84	M.H.Kania	Bombay	14/11/1969	01/05/1987	18/11/1992
85	K.Jagannatha Shetty	Karnataka	25/06/1970	01/05/1987	15/12/1991
86	L.M.Sharma	Patna	12/04/1973	25/10/1987	12/02/1993
87	M.N.Venkatachaliah	Karnataka	06/11/1975	05/10/1987	10/25/1994
88	S.Ranganathan	Delhi		05/10/1987	10/30/1992
89	N.D.Ojha	All	03/09/1971	18/01/1988	1/19/1991
90	S.R.Pandian	Madras	02/08/1975	14/12/1988	3/13/1994
91	T.K.Thommen, Dr.	Kerala	09/05/1975	14/12/1988	9/26/1993
92	A.M.Ahmadi	Guj.	02/09/1976	14/12/1988	3/25/1997
93	K.N.Saikia	Gauhati	12/02/1979	14/12/1988	3/1/1991
94	Kuldip Singh	Bar		14/12/1988	1/1/1997
95	J.S.Verma	M.P.	12/09/1972	03/06/1989	1/18/1998
96	V.Ramaswami - II	Madras	31/01/1971	06/10/1989	15/02/1994
97	P.B.Sawant	Bombay	29/03/1973	06/10/1989	6/30/1995
98	N.M.Kasliwal	Raj.	15/06/1978	06/10/1989	04/04/1993
99	M.M.Punchhi	P & H	24/10/1979	06/10/1989	10/10/1998
100	K.Ramaswamy	A.P.	29/09/1982	06/10/1989	7/13/1997
101	M.S.Fathima Beevi	Kerala	04/08/1983	06/10/1989	30/04/1992
102	K.Jayachandra Reddy	A.P.	07/03/1975	11/01/1990	7/15/1994
103	S.C.Agarwal	Raj.	15/06/1978	11/01/1990	9/5/1998
104	R.M.Sahai	All	27/01/1976	11/01/1990	6/25/1995
105	Yogeshwar Dayal	Delhi	28/02/1974	22/03/1991	11/18/1995
106	S.Mohan	Madras	27/02/1974	07/10/1991	2/11/1995
107	B.P.Jeevan Reddy	A.P.	17/07/1975	07/10/1991	3/14/1997
108	G.N.Ray	Cal	23/12/1976	07/11/1991	5/1/1998
109	A.S.Anand,Dr	J & K	26/05/1975	18/11/1991	11/1/2001
110	R.C.Patnaik	Orissa		20/11/1991	5/30/1992
111	N.P.Singh	Patna	12/04/1973	15/06/1992	12/25/1996
112	S.P.Bharucha	Bombay	19/09/1977	01/07/1992	5/6/2002
113	N.Venkatachala	Karnataka	28/11/1977	01/07/1992	7/3/1995
114	M.K.Mukherjee	Cal.	17/06/1977	14/12/1993	12/1/1998
115	Faizan-Uddin	MP	27/11/1978	14/12/1993	2/5/1997
116	B.L.Hansaria	Gauhati	12/02/1979	14/12/1993	12/25/1996
117	S.C.Sen	Cal	20/08/1982	11/06/1994	12/21/1997
118	K.S.Paripoornan	Kerala	23/12/1982	11/06/1994	6/12/1997
119	S.B.Majmudar	Guj.	03/10/1978	19/09/1994	8/20/2000
120	Sujata V.Manohar	Bombay	23/01/1978	08/11/1994	8/28/1999
121	G.T.Nanavati	Guj.	19/07/1979	06/03/1995	2/17/2000

Annexure 2

Sl.	Judge Name	PHC	Date HCJ	Date SCJ	Date Retd.
122	S.Saghir Ahmed	All	02/11/1981	06/03/1995	7/1/2000
123	K.Venkataswami	Madras	24/07/1983	06/03/1995	9/19/1999
124	B.N.Kirpal	Delhi	20/11/1979	11/09/1995	11/8/2002
125	G.B.Pattanaik	Orissa	01/06/1983	11/09/1995	12/19/2002
126	S.P.Kurdukar	Bombay	25/04/1978	29/03/1996	1/16/2000
127	K.T.Thomas	Kerala	12/08/1985	29/03/1996	1/30/2002
128	M.Jagannadha Rao	A.P.	29/09/1982	21/03/1997	12/2/2000
129	V.N.Khare	All	25/06/1983	21/03/1997	5/2/2004
130	D.P.Wadhwa	Delhi	12/08/1983	21/03/1997	5/5/2000
131	M.Srinivasan	Madras		25/09/1997	1/12/2002
132	S.R.Babu	Karnataka	19/02/1988	25/09/1997	6/1/2004
133	A.P.Misra	All	24/04/1984	04/12/1997	9/1/2001
134	S.M.Quadri	A.P.	11/07/1986	04/12/1997	4/5/2003
135	M.B.Shah	Guj.	28/01/1983	09/12/1998	9/25/2003
136	D.P.Mohapatra	Orissa	18/11/1983	09/12/1998	8/3/2002
137	U.C.Banerjee	Cal	09/01/1984	09/12/1998	11/18/2002
138	R.C.Lahoti	M.P.	03/05/1988	09/12/1998	11/1/2005
139	N.Santosh Hegde	Bar		08/01/1999	6/16/2005
140	R.P.Sethi	J & K	30/05/1986	08/01/1999	7/7/2002
141	S.N.Phukan	Gauhati	11/10/1985	28/01/1999	4/1/2002
142	Doraiswamy Raju	Karnataka	14/06/1990	28/01/2000	7/2/2004
143	Y.K.Sabharwal	Delhi	17/11/1986	28/01/2000	1/14/2007
144	Ruma Pal	Cal	06/08/1990	28/01/2000	6/3/2006
145	S.N.Variava	Bombay	21/11/1986	15/03/2000	11/8/2005
146	S.V.Patil	Karnataka	29/03/1990	15/03/2000	1/12/2005
147	K.G.Balakrishnan	Kerala	26/09/1985	08/06/2000	5/12/2010
148	Brijesh Kumar	All	15/10/1984	19/10/2000	6/10/2004
149	B.N.Agarwal	Patna	17/11/1986	19/10/2000	10/15/2009
150	P.Venkatarama Reddi	A.P.	16/03/1990	17/08/2001	8/10/2005
151	Ashok Bhan	P & H	15/06/1990	17/08/2001	10/2/2008
152	Arijit Pasayat	Orissa	20/03/1989	19/10/2001	5/10/2009
153	B.P.Singh	Patna	09/03/1987	14/12/2001	7/9/2007
154	D.M.Dharmadhikari	M.P.	24/03/1989	05/03/2002	8/14/2005
155	H.K.Sema	Gauhati	24/05/1989	09/04/2002	6/1/2008
156	S.B.Sinha	Patna	03/09/1987	03/10/2002	8/8/2009
157	Arun Kumar	Delhi	13/07/1990	03/10/2002	4/12/2006
158	B.N.Srikrishna	Bombay	30/07/1990	03/10/2002	5/21/2006
159	A.R.Lakshmanan	Madras	14/06/1990	31/07/2002	3/22/2007
160	G.P.Mathur	All	06/07/1990	20/12/2002	1/19/2008
161	S.H.Kapadia	Bombay	08/10/1991	18/12/2003	9/29/2012
162	Ashok K.Mathur	Raj.	13/03/1985	07/06/2004	8/7/2008

Annexure 2

Sl.	Judge Name	PHC	Date HCJ	Date SCJ	Date Retd.
163	C.K.Thakker	Guj.	21/06/1990	07/06/2004	11/10/2008
164	Tarun Chatterjee	Cal	06/08/1990	27/08/2004	1/14/2010
165	P.K.I.Balasubramanyan	Kerala	04/06/1992	27/08/2004	8/28/2007
166	P.P.Naolekar	M.P.	15/06/1992	27/08/2004	6/29/2008
167	Altamas Kabir	Cal	06/08/1990	09/09/2005	7/19/2013
168	R.N.Raveendharan	A.P.	22/02/1993	09/09/2005	10/15/2011
169	Dalveer C.Bhandari	Delhi	19/03/1991	28/10/2005	10/1/2012
170	Lokeshwar S.Panta	H.P.	20/08/1991	03/02/2006	4/23/2009
171	D.K.Jain	Delhi	19/03/1991	10/04/2006	25/01/2013
172	Markandey Katju	All	30/11/1991	10/04/2006	9/20/2011
173	H.S.Bedi	P & H	15/03/1991	12/01/2007	9/5/2011
174	V.S.Sirpurkar	Bombay	09/11/1992	12/01/2007	8/22/2011
175	B.Sudershan Reddy	A.P.	02/05/1995	12/01/2007	7/8/2011
176	P.Sathasivam	Madras	08/01/1996	21/08/2007	4/27/2014
177	G.S.Singhvi	Raj.	20/07/1990	12/11/2007	12/12/2013
178	Aftab Alam	Patna	27/07/1990	12/11/2007	4/19/2013
179	J.M.Panchal	Guj.	28/10/1994	12/11/2007	10/6/2011
180	Dr.M.K.Sharma	Gauhati	10/01/1994	09/04/2008	08/09/2011
181	Cyriac Joseph	Kerala	06/07/1994	07/07/2008	28/01/2012
182	A.K. Ganguly	Patna	10/01/1994	17/12/2008	03/02/2012
183	R.M. Lodha	Raj.	31/01/1994	17/12/2008	28/09/2014
184	H.L.Dattu	Karnataka	18/12/1995	17/12/2008	03/12/2015
185	Deepak Verma	M.P.	15/12/1994	11/05/2009	28/08/2012
186	Dr.B.S.Chauhan	All	05/04/1995	11/05/2009	02/07/2014
187	A.K.Patnaik	Orissa	13/01/1994	17/11/2009	03/06/2014
188	T.S.Thakur	J & K	16/02/1994	17/11/2009	04/01/2017
189	K.S.Radhakrishnan	Kerala	17/05/1995	17/11/2009	15/05/2014
190	S.S.Nijjar	P & H	08/04/1996	17/11/2009	07/06/2014
191	Swatanter Kumar	Delhi	10/11/1994	18/12/2009	31/12/2012
192	C.K.Prasad	Patna	08/11/1994	08/02/2010	15/07/2014
193	H.L.Gokhale	Bombay	20/01/1994	30/04/2010	10/03/2014
194	Ms.G. S. Mishra	Patna	16/03/1994	30/04/2010	28/04/2014
195	Anil R. Dave	Guj.	18/09/1995	30/04/2010	19/11/2016

PHC Permanent High Court
HCJ Appt. as High Court Judge
SCJ Appt. as Supreme Court Judge
DNA Data Not Available

Annexure 3
Hon'ble Judges according to Member of Bench

Sl. No.	Judge Name	JOC	Sign.	Order	Conc	Distng.	Mem. Ben
1	Arijit Pasayat	2092	461	105	3	0	2661
2	K.Ramaswamy	295	789	1172	10	6	2272
3	S.B.Sinha	1417	536	176	1	0	2130
4	J.C.Shah	617	1159	1	55	13	1845
5	G.B.Pattanaik	266	926	153	2	0	1347
6	P.B.Gajendragadkar	432	759	0	34	1	1226
7	K.N.Wanchoo	312	836	0	31	5	1184
8	M.Hidayatullah	363	653	0	54	21	1091
9	S.P.Bharucha	218	520	246	7	0	991
10	K.S.Hegde	415	512	1	33	3	964
11	S.M.Sikri	256	614	0	79	2	951
12	Kuldip Singh	266	518	139	7	1	931
13	A.N.Grover	307	572	1	34	0	914
14	K.Subha Rao	276	557	0	36	36	905
15	S.R.Babu	354	460	88	1	0	903
16	Syed M.Fazal Ali	480	381	10	27	2	900
17	Tarun Chatterjee	184	414	247	1	0	846
18	O.Chinnappa Reddy	340	452	23	19	2	836
19	K.G.Balakrishnan	175	350	305	1	0	831
20	R.S.Pathak	264	492	33	27	2	818
21	P.N.Bhagwati	353	391	36	24	10	814
22	Ranganath Misra	326	340	138	9	0	813
23	R.C.Lahoti	268	377	161	0	0	806
24	V.R.Krishna Iyer	410	324	16	35	8	793
25	Y.V.Chandrachud	360	370	14	42	2	788
26	S.H.Kapadia	217	457	114	0	0	788
27	A.N.Ray	271	434	0	64	6	775
28	V.N.Khare	124	437	212	1	0	774
29	A.P.Sen	223	448	71	12	9	763
30	B.P.Jeevan Reddy	323	291	133	12	1	760
31	N.Santosh Hegde	304	389	67	0	0	760
32	E.S.Venkataramiah	294	405	42	11	2	754
33	A.M.Ahmadi	220	366	155	2	4	747
34	S.C.Agrawal	230	413	93	8	2	746

Annexure 3

Sl. No.	Judge Name	JOC	Sign.	Order	Conc	Distng.	Mem. Ben
35	V.Ramaswami - I	240	499	1	3	3	746
36	A.S.Anand,Dr	150	367	207	8	0	732
37	M.M.Punchhi	129	416	168	2	1	716
38	R.S.Sarkaria	291	393	1	24	1	710
39	Y.K.Sabharwal	164	260	284	0	0	708
40	S.N.Variava	310	284	103	1	0	698
41	K.T.Thomas	268	318	107	3	0	696
42	Lokeshwar S.Panta	79	584	11	0	0	674
43	G.T.Nanavati	262	375	28	0	0	665
44	B.P.Sinha	128	476	0	55	0	659
45	D.A.Desai	295	307	11	21	4	638
46	J.M.Shelat	220	372	0	36	6	634
47	K.Jayachandra Reddy	303	257	65	7	0	632
48	Markandey Katju	129	452	49	1	0	631
49	A.K.Sarkar	174	385	0	40	22	621
50	S.Saghir Ahmed	135	422	57	1	0	615
51	B.N.Kirpal	149	307	157	2	0	615
52	P.Sathasivam	91	518	4	0	0	613
53	Sujata V.Manohar	178	338	88	1	0	605
54	C.K.Thakker	203	380	17	1	0	601
55	K.C.Das Gupta	155	417	0	26	3	601
56	Sabyasachi Mukharji	323	226	31	11	4	595
57	S.B.Majmudar	180	281	127	4	0	592
58	G.N.Ray	134	382	64	6	0	586
59	B.N.Agarwal	94	269	221	1	0	585
60	B.L.Hansaria	123	444	3	3	4	577
61	G.K.Mitter	147	374	0	50	5	576
62	M.K.Sharma,Dr.	89	476	8	0	0	573
63	H.R.Khanna	233	309	0	26	5	573
64	A.R.Lakshmanan, Dr.	225	333	13	0	0	571
65	Doraiswamy Raju	109	424	36	1	0	570
66	M.H.Beg	182	313	0	53	10	558
67	C.A.Vaidialingam	193	363	0	0	2	558
68	J.S.Verma	142	301	100	7	4	554
69	S.R.Dass	137	390	0	9	4	540
70	R.N.Raveendharan	163	248	125	1	0	537

Annexure 3

Sl. No.	Judge Name	JOC	Sign.	Order	Conc	Distng.	Mem. Ben
71	H.K.Sema	135	357	40	0	0	532
72	B.P.Singh	194	292	43	2	0	531
73	M.B.Shah	171	300	55	0	1	527
74	S.K.Das	148	347	0	18	4	517
75	D.P.Wadhwa	144	347	16	2	2	511
76	I.D.Dua	171	297	0	35	2	505
77	H.S.Bedi	93	368	38	0	0	499
78	S.V.Patil	154	284	61	0	0	499
79	J.R.Mudholkar	142	292	0	49	14	497
80	N.Venkatachala	82	398	7	2	0	489
81	M.N.Venkatachaliah	109	269	102	5	1	486
82	N.L.Untwalia	181	283	5	15	1	485
83	Ashok Bhan	150	287	48	0	0	485
84	N.R. Ayyangar	134	289	0	53	8	484
85	R.M.Sahai	153	269	52	6	4	484
86	P.Jaganmohan Reddy	149	296	0	35	0	480
87	J.L.Kapur	158	276	0	33	10	477
88	Ruma Pal	154	240	78	2	0	474
89	Raghuvar Dayal	129	309	0	18	14	470
90	N.P.Singh	118	310	17	3	0	448
91	A.C.Gupta	156	278	3	5	5	447
92	P.B.Sawant	131	250	57	5	1	444
93	R.S.Bachawat	161	260	0	11	7	439
94	N.H.Bhagwati	118	309	0	6	2	435
95	K.K.Mathew	130	270	0	19	14	433
96	D.P.Mohapatra	160	249	21	0	0	430
97	T.L.V. Ayyar	124	279	0	23	2	428
98	Altamas Kabir	192	192	41	0	0	425
99	S.M.Quadri	127	214	76	2	0	419
100	M.K.Mukherjee	134	254	30	0	0	418
101	K.Venkataswami	125	261	31	1	0	418
102	S.Ranganathan	131	239	30	15	2	417
103	B.C.Ray	101	284	22	8	1	416
104	P.K.Goswami	156	248	0	4	1	409
105	L.M.Sharma	153	221	24	6	3	407

Annexure 3

Sl. No.	Judge Name	JOC	Sign.	Order	Conc	Distng.	Mem. Ben
106	G.P.Mathur	162	227	17	0	0	406
107	M.Jagannadha Rao	142	205	59	0	0	406
108	V.D.Tulzapurkar	154	218	5	18	4	399
109	A.D.Koshal	79	306	1	10	2	398
110	D.K.Jain	63	286	42	0	0	391
111	Vivian Bose	106	269	1	7	7	390
112	R.P.Sethi	157	229	4	0	0	390
113	V.S.Sirpurkar	114	256	16	0	0	386
114	S.Mohan	119	211	46	4	0	380
115	Dalveer C.Bhandari	111	235	31	1	0	378
116	Asok Kumar Ganguly	38	330	1	0	0	369
117	S.C.Sen	101	237	27	1	1	367
118	P.N.Shinghal	104	243	0	17	2	366
119	S.N.Phukan	78	283	5	0	0	366
120	V.Bhargava	125	229	0	10	2	366
121	G.L.Oza	83	257	19	5	0	364
122	A.Alagiriswami	133	215	0	14	2	364
123	Aftab Alam	43	302	8	0	0	353
124	M.M.Dutt	109	235	5	3	0	352
125	Syed Jafar Imam	65	282	0	4	0	351
126	Jaswant Singh	94	242	0	10	2	348
127	K.S.Paripoornan	66	273	3	3	1	346
128	K.N.Singh	84	224	36	1	0	345
129	R.B.Misra	73	263	0	4	0	340
130	U.C.Banerjee	125	194	19	0	0	338
131	Ashok K.Mathur	111	171	54	0	0	336
132	Brijesh Kumar	87	229	19	0	0	335
133	V.B.Eradi	49	275	4	4	0	332
134	S.R.Pandian	134	148	46	3	0	331
135	K.Jagannatha Shetty	155	149	17	8	0	329
136	N.M.Kasliwal	122	195	8	3	1	329
137	P.S.Kailasam	90	221	0	8	3	322
138	M.C.Mahajan	109	195	0	9	5	318
139	Cyriac Joseph	0	307	1	0	0	308
140	M.H.Kania	96	196	12	2	0	306

Annexure 3

Sl. No.	Judge Name	JOC	Sign.	Order	Conc	Distng.	Mem. Ben
141	A.P.Mishra	73	205	27	0	0	305
142	S.P.Kurdukar	73	217	15	0	0	305
143	P.P.Naolekar	48	239	10	0	0	297
144	B.K.Mukherjea	84	196	0	12	2	294
145	D.M.Dharmadhikari	83	205	4	0	0	292
146	D.G.Palekar	88	167	0	34	2	291
147	G.S.Singhvi	42	244	4	0	0	290
148	A.Varadarajan	56	216	1	5	6	284
149	Yogeshwar Dayal	130	111	13	25	1	280
150	B.Sudershan Reddy	52	219	3	0	0	274
151	S.Natarajan	90	166	11	2	0	269
152	Faizanuddin	60	203	4	0	0	268
153	P.Venkatarama Reddi	83	158	18	1	0	260
154	Arun Kumar	53	199	3	0	0	255
155	P.K.I.Balasubramanyan	83	165	2	0	0	250
156	A.N.Sen	31	191	1	16	2	241
157	B.N.Srikrishna	85	150	4	0	0	239
158	N.D.Ojha	38	184	4	4	0	230
159	B.Jagannath Das	65	157	0	0	5	227
160	M.P.Thakkar	96	89	37	3	2	227
161	J.M.Panchal	46	164	4	0	0	214
162	M.S.Fathima Beevi	46	162	1	3	0	212
163	V.Khalid	53	147	1	7	0	208
164	H.L.Dattu	40	155	3	0	0	198
165	Rajendra Mal Lodha	72	116	0	0	0	188
166	Baharul Islam	27	151	1	1	3	183
167	M.Srinivasan	62	101	10	1	0	174
168	V.Ramaswami - II	30	137	1	0	1	169
169	Ghulam Hasan	27	133	0	5	0	165
170	T.K.Thommen	65	85	12	2	1	165
171	M.Patanjali Sastri	53	93	0	12	1	159
172	K.N.Saikia	32	112	8	0	0	152
173	N.C. Aiyar	39	99	0	3	1	142
174	S.N.Dwivedi	42	67	0	19	1	129
175	Deepak Verma	22	96	1	0	0	119

Annexure 3

Sl. No.	Judge Name	JOC	Sign.	Order	Conc	Distng.	Mem. Ben
176	D.P.Madon	37	73	0	2	0	112
177	B.S.Chauhan,Dr.	25	81	3	0	0	109
178	Saiyid Fazal Ali	41	53	0	7	3	104
179	P.Govinda Menon	15	54	0	0	0	69
180	R.Satyanarayan Raju	15	51	0	0	0	66
181	A.K.Mukherjea	17	42	0	6	0	65
182	H.J.Kania	23	35	0	3	1	62
183	K.S.Radhakrishnan	14	43	0	0	0	57
184	S.S.Nijjar	18	29	5	0	0	52
185	R.C.Patnaik	1	41	0	0	0	42
186	A.K.Patnaik	7	30	2	0	0	39
187	S.C.Roy	4	20	0	4	0	28
188	T.S.Thakur	11	14	1	0	0	26
189	Swatanter Kumar	8	17	0	0	0	25
190	C.K.Prasad	4	12	0	0	0	16
191	Ramachander Naik	1	3	0	0	0	4
192	K. Siddiqui	1	3	0	0	0	4
193	Ms.G. S. Mishra	0	3	0	0	0	3
194	Anil R. Dave	0	3	0	0	0	3
195	H.L.Gokhale	0	1	0	0	0	1

JOC Judgement of Court
Sign. Signatory
Conc. Concurring
Distg. Dissenting
Mem. Ben. Member Bench

Annexure 4
Hon'ble Judges from High Courts

High Court	Sl. No.	Hon'ble Justice
Andhra Pradesh		
	1	Ramachander Naik
	2	Khaleeluzzaman Siddiqui
	3	R.Satyanarayan Raju
	4	P.Jaganmohan Reddy
	5	O.Chinnappa Reddy
	6	K.Ramaswamy
	7	K.Jayachandra Reddy
	8	B.P.Jeevan Reddy
	9	M.Jagannadha Rao
	10	S.M.Quadri
	11	P.Venkatarama Reddi
	12	B.Sudershan Reddy
Allahabad		
	1	Ghulam Hasan
	2	K.N.Wanchoo
	3	Raghuvar Dayal
	4	V.Bhargava
	5	M.H.Beg
	6	S.N.Dwivedi
	7	R.S.Pathak
	8	R.B.Misra
	9	K.N.Singh
	10	N.D.Ojha
	11	R.M.Sahai
	12	S.Saghir Ahmed
	13	V.N.Khare
	14	A.P.Misra
	15	Brijesh Kumar
	16	G. P. Mathur
	17	Markandey Katju
	18	B.S.Chauhan Dr.

Annexure 4

Bombay

1	H.J.Kania
2	Vivian Bose
3	N.H.Bhagwati
4	P.B.Gajendragadkar
5	M.Hidayatullah
6	K.C.Das Gupta
7	J.C.Shah
8	J.R.Mudholkar
9	J.M.Shelat
10	D.G.Palekar
11	Y.V.Chandrachud
12	V.D.Tulzapurkar
13	D.P.Madon
14	M.H.Kania
15	P.B.Sawant
16	S.P.Bharucha
17	Sujata V.Manohar
18	S.P.Kurdukar
19	S.N.Variava
20	B.N.Srikrishna
21	S.H.Kapadia
22	V.S.Sirpurkar
23	H.L.Gokhale

Calcutta

1	B.K.Mukherjea
2	S.R.Dass
3	A.K.Sarkar
4	R.S.Bachawat
5	G.K.Mitter
6	A.N.Ray
7	A.K.Mukherjea
8	A.C.Gupta
9	A.N.Sen
10	Sabyasachi Mukharji
11	B.C.Ray
12	M.M.Dutt

Annexure 4

	13	G.N.Ray
	14	M.K.Mukherjee
	15	S.C.Sen
	16	U.C.Banerjee
	17	Ruma Pal
	18	Tarun Chatterjee
	19	Altamas Kabir
	20	Asok Kumar Ganguly
Delhi		
	1	H.R.Khanna
	2	S.Ranganathan
	3	Yogeshwar Dayal
	4	B.N.Kirpal
	5	D.P.Wadhwa
	6	Y.K.Sabharwal
	7	Arun Kumar
	8	Dalveer C.Bhandarı
	9	D.K.Jain
	10	Swatanter Kumar
Gauhati		
	1	P.K.Goswami
	2	Baharul Islam
	3	K.N.Saikia
	4	B.L.Hansaria
	5	S.N.Phukan
	6	H.K.Sema
	7	Dr.M.K.Sharma
Gujarat		
	1	P.N.Bhagwati
	2	D.A.Desai
	3	M.P.Thakkar
	4	A.M.Ahmadi
	5	S.B.Majmudar
	6	G.T.Nanavati
	7	M.B.Shah
	8	C.K.Thakker
	9	J.M.Panchal

Annexure 4

	10	Anil R. Dave
Himachal Pradesh		
	1	Lokeshwar S.Panta
Jammu & Kashmir		
	1	Syed M.Fazal Ali
	2	Jaswant Singh
	3	A.S.Anand,Dr
	4	R.P.Sethi
	5	T.S.Thakur
Karnataka		
	1	K.S.Hegde
	2	E.S.Venkataramiah
	3	K.Jagannatha Shetty
	4	M.N.Venkatachaliah
	5	N.Venkatachala
	6	S.R.Babu
	7	Doraiswamy Raju
	8	S.V.Patil
	9	R.V.Raveendran
	10	H.L.Dattu
Kerala		
	1	C.A.Vaidialingam
	2	K.K.Mathew
	3	V.R.Krishna Iyer
	4	V.B.Fradi
	5	T.K.Thommen, Dr.
	6	M.S.Fathima Beevi
	7	K.S.Paripoornan
	8	K.T.Thomas
	9	K.G.Balakrishnan
	10	P.K.I.Balasubramanyan
	11	Cyriac Joseph
	12	K.S.Radhakrishnan
Madhya Pradesh		
	1	A.P.Sen
	2	G.L.Oza

Annexure 4

	3	J.S.Verma
	4	Faizan-Uddin
	5	R.C.Lahoti
	6	D.M.Dharmadhikari
	7	P.P.Naolekar
	8	Deepak Verma
Madras		
	1	M.Patanjali Sastri
	2	N.Chandrashekar Aiyar
	3	T.L.Venkatarama Ayyar
	4	P.Govinda Menon
	5	K.Subha Rao
	6	N.Rajgopala Ayyangar
	7	V.Ramaswami - I
	8	A.Alagiriswami
	9	P.S.Kailasam
	10	A.Varadarajan
	11	V.Khalid
	12	S.Natrajan
	13	S.R.Pandian
	14	V.Ramaswami - II
	15	S.Mohan
	16	K.Venkataswami
	17	M.Srinivasan
	18	A.R.Lakshmanan
	19	P.Sathasivam
Orissa		
	1	B.Jagannath Das
	2	Ranganath Misra
	3	R.C.Patnaik
	4	G.B.Pattanaik
	5	D.P.Mohapatra
	6	Arijit Pasayat
	7	A.K.Patnaik

Annexure 4

Punjab & Haryana

1	M.C.Mahajan
2	J.L.Kapur
3	A.N.Grover
4	I.D.Dua
5	R.S.Sarkaria
6	A.D.Koshal
7	M.M.Punchhi
8	Ashok Bhan
9	H.S.Bedi
10	S.S.Nijjar

Patna

1	Saiyid Fazal Ali
2	B.P.Sinha
3	Syed Jafar Imam
4	S.K.Das
5	N.L.Untwalia
6	L.M.Sharma
7	N.P.Singh
8	B.N.Agarwal
9	B.P.Singh
10	S.B.Sinha
11	Aftab Alam
12	C.K.Prasad
13	Ms.Gyan Sudha Mishra

Rajasthan

1	P.N.Shinghal
2	N.M.Kasliwal
3	S.C.Agarwal
4	Ashok K.Mathur
5	G.S.Singhvi
6	Rajendra Mal Lodha

Bar

1	S.M.Sikri
2	S.C.Roy
3	Kuldip Singh
4	N.Santosh Hegde

Annexure 5
Hon'ble Chief Justices and Judges who resigned

Hon'ble Chief Justice

1. K. Subba Rao
2. R.S. Pathak

Hon'ble Justice

1. J.R. Mudholkar
2. J.M. Shelat
3. K.S. Hegde
4. A.N. Grover
5. H.R. Khanna
6. Bahrul Islam

Annexure 6
Hon'ble Chief Justices and Judges who expired in office

Hon'ble Chief Justice

1. H.J. Kania
2. Sabyasachi Mukharji

Hon'ble Justice

1. P. Govind Menon
2. R. Satyanarayan Raju
3. S.C. Roy
4. S.N. Dwivedi
5. A.K. Mukherjea
6. Syed M. Fazal Ali
7. Yogeshwar Dayal
8. R.C. Patnaik
9. M. Srinivasan

Annexure 7
Hon'ble Ad-hoc Judges

Hon'ble Justice

1. Ramchander Naik 28.08.1950 to 30.12.1950
2. Khaleeluzzaman Naik 28.08.1950 to 30.12.1950
3. Vivan Bose 09.09.1957 to 30.09.1958
4. T.L.Veankatarama Ayyar 11.03.1961 to 30.04.1961 & 20.12.1961 to 06.05.1962
5. K. Jayachandra Reddy 15.07.1994 to 14.07.1995

Annexure 8

Judgements referred, considered etc. in more than 50 Judgements

Sl	Appellant	Respondent	Citation	Follow Up
1	Maneka Gandi	Union of India	(1978) 2 SCR 0621	136
2	Bengal Imm. Co.Ltd.	State of Bihar	(1955) 2 SCR 0603	101
3	H.H.Kesavananda Bharti	State of Kerala	(1973)Supp. SCR 0001	91
4	A.K.Gopalan	State of TN	(1950) SCR 0088	88
5	Bachan Singh	State of Punjab	(1980) 2 SCC 0684	88
6	R.K.Dalmiya	Jus S.R.Tenulkar	(1959) SCR 0279	87
7	Chiranjital Choudhary	Union of India	(1950) SCR 0869	82
8	R.D.Shetty	IAAI	(1979) 3 SCR 1014	80
9	D.S.Nakara	Union of India	(1983) 2 SCR 0165	77
10	Com.of H.R.E.	L.T..S.Shummir	(1954) SCR 1005	71
11	Purshotamlal Dhingra	Union of India	(1958) SCR 0828	70
12	Stat of West Bengal	Anwar Ali Sarkar	(1952) SCR 0284	70
13	R.C. Cooper	Union of India	(1970) 3 SCR 0530	66
14	State of T.N.	Gannon Dunkerley & Co. Ltd	(1959) SCR 0379	66
15	State of Bihar	K. Singh	(1952) SCR 0889	66
16	State of Tamil Nadu	V.G.Rao	(1952) SCR 0597	64
17	A.K.Kraipak	Union of India	(1970) 1 SCR 0457	64
18	State of Maharashtra	F.N.Balsara	(1951) SCR 0682	63
19	Shamsher Singh	State of Punjab	(1975) 1 SCR 0814	62
20	Ajay Hasia	K.M.Sehravardi	(1981) 2 SCR 0079	60
21	DR Class II Eng.Asn.	State of Mah.	(1990) 2 SCR 0900	60
22	Exp.News. Pvt. Ltd.	Union of India	(1959) SCR 0012	58
23	Aut. Tpt. Raj.Ltd.	State of Raj.	(1963) 1 SCR 0491	55
24	S.P.Gupta	Union of India	(1982) 2 SCR 0365	55
25	State of Maharashtra	UMotors (I) Ltd.	(1953) SCR 1069	54
26	In Re.Delhi Law Act, 1912		(1951) SCR 0747	54

Annexure 9
Parameters of analysis

A judgment can be related to in another judgment on one of the following parameters

- Affirmed
- Applied
- Distinguished
- Doubted
- Explained
- Followed
- Limited
- Not Good Law
- Obiter
- Over Ruled
- Per-Incurium
- Referred
- Relied on

Annexure 10
Parameters of Opinion

An opinion delivered by a Hon'ble Judge for analysis falls within one of the following parameters:

- Concurring in part with Dissenting
- Concurring in part with Judgment of Court
- Concurring in part with Majority
- Concurring with Dissenting
- Concurring with Majority
- Dissenting
- Dissenting in part
- Judgment of Court
- Majority
- Observation
- Order
- Signatory
- Signatory with Concurring
- Signatory with Dissenting

How data accumulation helps in national growth...

- Persons of institution related and affected by technological advancement come to understand the data generation process,
- By proper structuring the data, a value is extracted by organization generating data
- This value is transformed in the form of information
- The information is disseminated and properly interpreted.
- Information when applied appropriately generates knowledge
- Knowledge helps in decision making process
- Accumulation of correct decisions leads to learning and wisdom.
- Organizational wisdom culminates and provides integrity and strength to institution which helps the nation to move forward...

Law Information Center (LawInC)

Law Information Center (LawInC) was registered as a society under the Societies Registration Act, 1860 on 19.12.1994, with the objective to collect, analyze, process, disseminate updated information and data relating to law. LawInC has contributed its little under the proficient guidance of former Judges of Supreme Court of India, Law Minister of India, Solicitor General and Addl. Solicitor General's of India and several others. LawInC launched the first legal website in India on 07.11.1996 (Hon'ble Justice M.M. Punchi) and has silently, steadfastly and determinedly continued its activities ever since.

Executive Committee 2009 -2012

Chairman	Arijit Pasayat J.
Vice Chairman	Altaf Ahmed
Vice Chairman	R.N.Trivedi
Vice Chairman	S.S.Javlli
President	Aruneshwar Gupta
Vice President	V.K.Agarwal
Vice President	R.Santhaan Krishnan
Vice President	Jitendra M.Sharma
Secretary General	Bijan Ghosh
Asst. Secretary Gen.	Abani Kumar Sahu
Treasurer	Kumar Kartikay
Asst. Treasurer	Anish Dayal
Member	A.Marirputham
Member	P.S.Narasimha
Member	K.P. Kylasanath
Member	Gopal Singh
Member	Manoj Das
Member	Nikhilesh Ramchandran
Member	Nikhil Goel
Member	C.D.Singh
Member	Asha Nair
Member	Rajesh Srivastava